Pecking Away at the Madonna

Pecking Away at the Madonna

Joy Rosenberg

Petunia Press Books
Los Angeles

© 2016 by Joy Rosenberg

All rights reserved.

ISBN 978-0-692-76821-1

Produced in the United States of America

Cover artwork and layout:
Darrin Brenner - D. Brenner Art & Design

www.petuniapressbooks.com

To my mother and father

Contents

Magic Swirling Ship	9
Suitable for Gravy	11
Within a Deafening Whisper	12
Sanna, at one a.m.	13
Hovering Over a Spotless Sink	15
Coming Home to a Supposedly Empty House	16
My Aunt Sits and Smokes	18
Breasts	20
May in Massachusetts	21
Jeans	22
Walking With Yaz	24
Traveling	25
Goals for the Old Writer Becoming New Again	26
American Woman	28
Siddhartha	29
Lowell, Massachusetts	30
Because If	31
Contained in a Mist	32
Protection	34
Archaeology	35
In so many ways we are given rebirths	37
You leave. I look up	38
It's dark, naked	39
Gethsemane	40
Premeditation	41
This Dream Never Ends	42

First Day in San Francisco	43
Thank You, Diane di Prima, For Writing in Questions	44
Reckoning	45
Waking up in Samuel Taylor State Park, Surrounded by Redwoods	46
Stray Cat on Speedball Alley	48
Venice Is a Vampire	49
The Trees at the End of Westminster	50
Sestina	51
Notes on a Sharon Olds Reading	53
New New Jersey Blues	54
back door woman	56
Yerma	57
Journeywoman	58
An Exceptional Poem	60
(acknowledgement to Robert Hayden)	61

Pecking Away at the Madonna

Magic Swirling Ship

pajamagirl
blue beret invisible
eyes pierced navel
and nose
bare feet snake
bracelet crawls as the
Cheshire cat grins flow from her lips
in curls

tenseboy wears a
goateed smile, lips
and fingers love to smoke
pounces, hanging on the edge
like a fish
out of water, flopping
out of breath, talking
of graphics, of drums
beats, without his shirt, his
bare chest waves
of hair cascade
in blonde longlong gloats

smilegirl wanders
in, swings out
chairs like a wave
eat us like amoebas
and blondegirl wears black
and blue, goes out
with hairboy daddy-o
for beer, cheapest they can find
driving through the swims of their minds
dredlockpolyesterboy loots
up, looks down
offers to the girl from that other town
he digs all the way a new spaceygirl
take a drag on this to get into her world

girl from that other town puts
her head back, looks around
the room sees straight lines,
dry and paper thin
boy with coffeebrownsquintyeyes, soft
creamyspun ringlets of mochasilk shivers
deliciously to the milkyflow of
spilled Marleydips and grooves
pocket full of posies and ashes,
ashes burned his thigh
darkhaired Jewish Jesus ascends, spins
astrophysicist prophecies
and burnboy with the diablocuriousmile
completes no-progression, hopeless nightmare
contradictions
hairboy and blueblackblond return
edgeboy rolls a magic wand
dredboy and quietgirl disappear
stranger girls have seen bended lines
on the edge of rolling stones
collapsing, out
the door swings in
on itself

Suitable for Gravy

The fat on my body lies
like a layer of
thick heavy
waiting waiting conglomerating
under the pliable flesh
of my stomach, making it
a full-fledged belly.
A spindly, prickly, rubbery turkey, I am stuffed
with mashy, mushy breadcrumbs and drippings
saturated and soggy.
My insides:
suitable for gravy.

Luscious long licking, my tongue
wakes it to fester –
up from my neck,
creeping, creasing, rolling.
Under my skin
it lays bubbles blubbles bounces
disappearing at night and drying…
Day looks down at me
through nightclothing concealing
the afterbreakfast moisty meatloaf morning.
Once taut and firm
I shake jiggle sway splash
with gastric chyme
dibbley-dribbling
from my chin, my gluttonous
chins, procreating
with folds and grins

Someday I will boil inside,
knowing it would drain from me if I
opened up and poured it out.

Within a Deafening Whisper

Within a deafening whisper I curl
around in myself,
secretly wishing the rain inside.
Will you still be here when it stops,
in the damp, sentient cool of humid sheets,
all of you
streaming
down my legs
into a steaming
puddle at my feet?

This heavy flower
a burden in my head,
thumping and blooming as you stir.
With orchid breath
I breathe the question:
Have you awoken to its desperate need
or to the full, round drops of morning?

Sanna, at one a.m.

Sanna, at one a.m.
comes home from
the espresso bar downtown,
plops in the chair,
    releases her hair

It spills like cream
over her shoulders,
her shirt
soaked through with smoke,
soaked through with smoke.

Just another day, sitting,
sipping and talking
and giggling at the guy behind the counter.
He made us peppermint ginseng tea
and watched, saying nothing
as you coated the sides of your cup
with honey to the sounds of R.E.M.,
pumping through the grinds of afternoon.
Cuyahoga, cicada summer hung heavy,
the humidity holding us in the
thin strands of steam that
slithered up to the ceiling.
The sun burned through the storefront window
as we melted into the saturated grounds of night.

The bounce of beans was an alarm after hours.
Like lemmings they ran from the scoop,
pelted the glass jar and collided
like charged ions.
When the chairs were up on the tables except ours,
the manager told us to
return our cups and
come back tomorrow.

Sanna, when you are home at one a.m.,
does what lasted lucidly through the erasure of several
overrated hours
eventually dissipate?
Do you care that, later, I settled
for sitting on the freezer in the back store room,
me and the guy,
with his apron slung over the chair,
watching and tasting thick ribbons of smoke?

I wanted you to somehow find your way back there
and react in a normal, jealous sort of way
as I let him stuff coffee beans in my mouth,
by the handful.

Hovering Over a Spotless Sink

Hovering
over a spotless sink,
tweezing, twisting, brushing
I inadvertently dropped a bobby pin
on the bathroom floor.
And in the hasty routine of
not really caring for
one pin,
down sprung another;
it hopped like a grasshopper from my hand
and the loss of the two combined became
much more exasperatingly unbearable than
the single loss of
the first.

So I ventured down
under the sink
to the graveyard of
vanity mishaps and angry frustrations.
There was a blue comb,
discarded in someone's disgust
There was the coveted hair,
still lingering in chromosomal threads
wedged between teeth in tangled clumps
of deathly reminder
sheeting the hard tile
skirting the porcelain base
a network dry as bone dust, brittle as straw.

I left it there to remain
hidden from view
below the point of
rinsing away,
washing clean.
They must have fallen beneath the ledge and
surely I must have some other bobby pins.

Coming Home to a Supposedly Empty House

Through the door, unbreathing,
you come.
A sigh, then
forced, inevitable
at the drawn drapes and
the must of a house
unopened for a day.
I lie in the back room,
half-drowned with the flu.

Your keys clink on the counter,
jacket unzips, water
from the faucet fills a glass.
Clock hand snaps an interval.

The floorboards groan with your weight
on their tender spots,
yielding to your tread—
    heavy-heeled clunks on linoleum,
    muffled swish on the worn rug plush
as you head upstairs.
The banister admits your grip, winces—
the broken joint where I had
tripped, running
up to my room, away
from where I had carved my name,
away from your anger.

You start up the stairs:
the roll of chair wheels on hardwood,
the squeak of the mattress edge.
I know the coat still rests on your shoulders.
Is it worth taking it off
to stare into the yard from the darkening window?

A few minutes later, as you head back down,
I want you to walk in the door again
so I can announce my presence.
But for now, I try to control my
twitching eyelids, feign sleep as if I might
disappear into the dust swirls in the
late-afternoon sun that fights,
fights against the drapes with
all its might.

As the wind kicks in
through the chimney,
a gust of cold charcoal fills my nose
and I wish you didn't have to
come back
into this room
to make a fire.

My Aunt Sits and Smokes

My aunt sits and smokes,
disguised in a peach velour jacket
and carefree blond hair,
a resemblance of my father
too long masked by
the sprawled writing:
"Ten inches of snow in Wyoming already."

"Why don't you move back east?"
he used to ask.
"I can't…their father…you know."
He knows.
Now.

Destiny toward the western skyline
like Cody he ventured into a
bleeding horizon preceding a night,
sharp and arid
under the stars.

He found her living as
a tangleweed,
dry, restless reeling beside the endless road of
western lineage.

They mentioned it had been three weeks
since they saw their father.
He wondered if that van
would reappear in his sister's driveway
now
that he was leaving.
He didn't ask, and she
didn't say.

Yellowstone's smell of
rotten eggs couldn't put them back
in the car. They raged

with rage deep as
sulphur pools, bleached as
animal bones
and, barely watching Old Faithful
(three times in a row),
they were quiet on the way home.
Around that time,
he was buying us souvenirs
in Jackson Hole.
Unshaven, speeding, tearing apart the seams
of the Continental Divide,
he made it to Denver.
With only five minutes to spare he fled
the bloodline sky while
earth still heaved with the thuds of her
freshly gaping wound.

His eyes are tired but
hers delight.
This summer is setting in the west.
Even he knows that,
now.

My aunt sits and smokes.
She's never dared to ask,
"Why don't you move
out west?"

Breasts

Mine are 18 years old
perfectly-fashioned tiny globes
tinged with rose
color and sweet to the lips.
Some may say they are really only six,
or seven,
but I knew they were there
before they opened up.

Right now they are warmth
they are sweetness and sex
they are words I can't speak,
hanging behind my dress.
Two cupsful of thick honey
loose enough to conform
viscous so as not to spill.
I can't think of the day they will become
heavy with drink,
low and slow with the pulls of gravity and age,
lined as my life stretches to extents.

So I've learned to forget
when I feared the firmness of cells
when I tried to starve it out before it would come.
I can make them disappear, I learned,
others could not possibly carve into
things that weren't there,
cancer that had never blossomed
like a flower atop my bones and ribs

It was only when I realized it had already budded
in my mind that I let myself grow,

    let myself go...

May in Massachusetts

Two days ago
I packed away my down coat
    the winter one with the furry hood,
    deep pockets and
    marshmallow sleeves
Today I dug it back up.
Walked outside, the rain was freezing,
    my nipples like hailstones
    my blood an icy river
I walked in pain
and shouted at the fog
    shouted at the sight of my own breath
    shouted and spat at the reflection of my puffy,
    teary eyes
When you talked to me later that evening
in the underground café,
you moved my coat aside and sat,
    not looking at my face.
And when I got up to leave, you
stared at my coat,
    the buttons and zips,
    the puff and fur
and tried to find me inside all that goose.
But I was already bundled well,
had swathed myself for the cold walk home.

Jeans

I have created a wonderful plan for you
—for me—
It is my history, my future,
rolled into one week,
when we stay behind in the quiet of their wake,
the dust from when they
skidded out of here
still settling on my heart,
which hangs from your bedpost,
dangling stolid like yesterday's jeans—
your shape still encoded,
molded to the likeness of your hips.

Earlier this evening I sat inside
a Dali, with whitewashed trees, bare
as naked ladies in winter,
silver clouds sailing a black sky.
I once put my hands in someone's cement imprint,
    wanted to stop on the street,
    take off my shoes and socks,
    stand in her footprints as well.
It would have been odd, then.
But is it right when my body still
occupies her space
and I lay naked in her carving
on my mattress?

I can almost make out
how I slept last night,
how closed shut I rocked in lullaby,
how stoic I slept in effigy.
I have always been this way and only wanted
someone to find me,

to put me on,
like you will,
like day-old jeans,
warm, wonderful denim,
growing cold as they hang
like a carcass
near your head.

Walking With Yaz

And we started walking,
well, sort of together, I mean,
I was going one way, and so was she,
and I blurted some comments about
this and that, and then,
although I had been blathering the whole time,
at a point she spoke her only words—
she said,
    "Our paths diverge."
Just like that,
with the long "i" and everything.
And although it really was the truth—
she was going in one direction, and I was, well,
going in another—
it was symbolic because, hell,
we were diverging
and I would have just kept on talking, but she,
she pointed it out,
and even waited for me to absorb
the impending separation.
And I kept going, alone,
thinking how much I would have liked
to be the type of person who said that,
and wondering: if she hadn't,
would I ever have shut up?

Traveling

A long time ago
she would have boarded the train,
Dorothy Parker in a
houndstooth wool suit.
Dark brown fedora,
wisps framing her face
bobbypins secure, a
sheer-stockinged leg
clasped to the other at the knee.

She is moving
She is traveling
My mother
with a gray suitcase,
clothes neatly folded,
fingernails trimmed in haste,
going where she dreamed of
painting them red.
She would have liked to light a cigarette
and, tasting smoke,
stare into the dark eyes of a stranger
over the muted green
of an olive that sinks slowly
through the deceptive clarity
of a thick martini.

Goals for the Old Writer Becoming New Again

Scansion, meter, rhythm, rhyme
Scansion, meter, rhythm, rhyme
I cannot make it work this time
I can't even think
dirty dishes to the sink.

I must burrow deeper,
not be scared to hear the thump
   of a pen about to burst,
   of a mind growing weaker
as I seek to quench my thirst.
Ignoring form to get to meaning,
meaning better but forming worse.
I never rhyme,
but it's come high time!
Shall I turn to Suess, make
   Bibbley
      Bobbley
         Bubbley juice?
To write like talks that I've just had
To write the words that were not said—
that's what I should be doing instead!
Learning merely to write
   not
Listening for the ear,
   not
Having the fear
of an unendearing ear

   the untrained ear
   that does not hear
   the pulse of the pen
   the throb of the ink
   the splatter of the work in vain
   over years,

Peeling back to convey
what I've wanted to say
Opinions, like skin, will flake off with the flay
Scansion, meter, rhythm, rhyme
Scansion, meter, rhythm, rhyme
I have to make it work this time
I have to make it worth
your time...
To hear me through the walls around the words
words I am speaking in voice on loan
to those who listen with ears not their own
ignoring the voices that may disturb.
It never seems like I'm doing it right
To get down on paper the half of it
I contort and twist to make it all fit
in, is it worth it to put up this fight?
When I am in life it's my pen that flies
and when I know what I love I'm a whore
with wanton spirit and a soul that's free
who wants to take you in under no guise
of pretentious skill, no holding back for
fear that I will kill my best poetry.

It's the thrill of the chase that makes me remember
   who I was before this fall,
     what I would have made without this wonder
   of what will make me a work
     of art
        after all

American Woman

They begin with thinking
something's wrong.

With calm lids you slowly blinked,
at regular intervals
I knew there was no machine inside of you

Figurina-Amerikana
you draw me like an icon
pulling black and white
into each other,
soaking and absorbing into gray.
Thoughts can pull menstrual lining
from the pit of my uterus to fire,
and can I weep?
I see myself, legs apart,
staring into the pit, ablaze,
and I wonder—
have I made it my duty not to?

But I talked about her today.
I see the scenes filling her head,
as she rips them, puffy and dry,
in tufts from her ears.
I have never seen her this way.
If I could take her scalp off in layers,
I would see, through the pastry-shell tissue,
worms gnawing away.

I would rather the Devil, hammering,
or her worst enemy.
But that's it. She's not getting better.

Siddhartha

but why question these
when it becomes an incision,
an act of murder, even,
to turn the page?
when it disturbs to create with pen
the unity of thought and word
to feel the rising of radiance,
the birth and decay of new life
in someone else's
futile goals?

a greater task:
not to waste
who might be working
unpretentiously by my side
with a face rising to meet
who does not pen
who does not think
who does not end

i am somewhere writing.

Lowell, Massachusetts

Chain links lie coiled in a bulky heap,
looped up like a rusting pile of shit.
Cement pathways guard the rage of the flushing deep
of the oil-slicked slime—This is it,
Jack Kerouac, your backyard: textile mills,
trainyards and chimneyed skies,
where stones with your words shoot up from strange hills
as if electrified, forced out by Gatsby's eyes.
Then onto your grave—flat, covered in weeds:
beer cans, flask, flag, "He honored life."
We, two young girls, looting your town for seeds
tread upon you and "Stella, honored wife"—
further flattening the grass path to your marbled face:
We are alive, and we've brought pens to this place.

Because If

My memory isn't

What scares me
What scares me

Is writing mine

Writing

Can turn on you

You know

What then

Contained in a Mist

All my poems begin with "I."
To say they end with you would be
too easy, these poems
that begin with no intent
to find you
and end you
by defining you with new words.

I know you too well not to know
your laugh could be
content or contempt.
I know you'd never pretend
it was solely
one or the other.

Where once there was reason,
there is obligation
Where once there was a heartbeat,
there is a time-bomb.
How did you flip the world like that
so my days are your days—
How did you make it
so you hang like a bat
in all of my doorways?

I torture myself with you
Your voice, your face
arcing over in orbit
like fallout from
The Big Bang.
Until, in cold fire, like water,
I approach my own beauty
like it is contained in a mist
of cold sparks
and coax into my arms a ball of flames
to roll after the one

who drove by today with your smile.
When I wake
and give myself to memory
I will write your name in ashes
on my bedside table.

For in our worst times
we must marvel at
our luck
to be alive.
At our worst,
we never sit outside closed doors
as we do in satisfaction.

Love,
how do you shine
over this poem
that reads like a translation?

Protection

Fortuitously, and sometimes out of duty, I ride the real night: those hollow but gestative hours of my pre-sleep fertility. The pregnancy of a strangely intimate encounter worming its way through, his warm fingers silting over my back, sifting through the used pages of my old journals. Life that used to be mine.

My body, quiet as a corpse, hides a mind hot as breath. She remembers her past, she remembers how she used to be before you. And how strong she was, and her promise to herself. Where there is night to be recaptured, she is busy squirming, begging to be taken. Or at least to be made to come.

Yes, there are meritorious moments. Moments when I am sure it does not matter who we are, together. I am finding my own voice so constantly loud, I am never really alone with you. She strains to come out and claim it, this thing she calls living, and is always disappointed to find me, rolled naked in the ditch of your armpit.

Ah, she is always here with us, the night muse, and each seed you misplant into latex, she sews into armor against you. Come as often as you wish, lie back wistfully and sleep. Go gentle into that good night, while my fingers rage, rage against the soft tendrils of your slumbering head.

It is she and I, once again, poets of darkness convening, taking inventory of what remains, gleaning what we will from never a fruitless encounter.

Sleeping, you seem like you are not quite ready for us.

Archaeology

All things dated, marked, recorded.
This date I mark the record
of my soul falling open,
ripe as a milky pod
separating in two palms.

We place pieces next to,
on top of
each other.
Our eyes erase the seams
to imagine the whole, uninterrupted.

In Israel,
Asa and I swim to the island off Dor.
As I bathe,
flashes of sunlight off the Mediterranean
knife the air.
An Ottoman bridge juts its stubborn
stone from the sand
begging not to be forgotten.
Tanninim, whisper the grains
I find him in a piscina,
thrice removed from life:
camera, goggles, glasses.
He is disappointed—
no dead fish.
Nothing to tell us
how things were.

Time will swallow us,
our structures with their empty eyes.
In our incidental graves, we will shift
and misplace ourselves from linear explanation.
We will be lied about in a re-creation,
our structures with their empty eyes,
which, when in life, would have told us all,

had we known how to examine their strata.

Later, alone on a walk through kibbutz at sunset,
I meet the panicked glint of a stray dog's eyes
as she barks with urgency at a chunk in the grass:
a dead lizard.

She wants to know why I'm not
doing anything about it.
What can I do?
It's a dead lizard.

If the eyes have it,
my soul expands limitlessly in all directions.
This is the last time the dog and I
will be the shapes we are,
and for a moment I wonder
just who is who.

In so many ways we are given rebirths

In so many ways we are given rebirths
to be that which we will
to meet and remeet
the souls we know and once knew

Vasudeva walks to the water
Vasudeva sits at the water
Vasudeva listens to the water
Vasudeva, the water

You leave. I look up

You leave. I look up
words in my French dictionary:
assez,
sèche.

I turn up, afloat.
Homeward, I think.
My body of water,
even the sea gets sick of me.
Drops me off, supine,
against a wall of sand.
Even my death will be a challenge.

Outward,
waves circle a tree.
A call to arms.
If not fly,
then swim.
If not swim,
then run.
If not run,
then walk.
If not walk,
then crawl
away
toward
from.

If not crawl,
then pull
yourself out.

It's dark, naked

It's dark, naked
this time of trouble, half
empty and draining

A dying, through waiting, comes,
mindful and heavy
tearlessness all streaming
to find you in the
out-froms
of poems, of days

How timelessness
becomes us
depends
if time spent apart
our lovelessness ends

I can make you
stark-nake you
wrap you up around
me where I stand
when we are through

But you never come out;
none of these poems ever has you in it.

Gethsemane

A girl-child,
nymphet
straggly and unforgiving
penchant to the wind,
element of earth and sky

I bear her
with knowledge of nothing,
aware of it All
My bodhisattva,
my transcendence into night
where the stuffiness of silence
and the dripping of dew
close in and refresh me

O sultry darkness,
sweet with honeysuckle sex,
wet with anticipation of the
blue-black rolling sky
I alone, feeding my newborn
to night,
child of selfish thoughts
saves me through sacrifice.

Woman-child,
never grow up
never grow old
never know the garden
never know the desperate prayer
never know paradise coated
with blackness,
erased for hours

If my mind survives,
I will make it to morning.

Premeditation

She is the wood, defying the carving knife.
Rounded, shape without name.

It always ends with a stain.
But I begin with a stain,
since that is where I am left behind,
drying as you dress and leave.

It always begins with a kiss.
But I end with a kiss, when I turn
my face and deny you,
and the event,
and the paralysis.

Feeling is a curse, a jab
in the wooden heart, jab in the
wooden thigh. As sharp as the absence of my
kiss, as permanently hard as the stain.

Why I write this without anger,
why I still wish to be polite,
why I walk past your front yard and
still think about knocking on the door.
Why I whittle,
re-carve you daily into my fresh new skin,
so I dry and fall off from being like a scab.

They hold hands across the table.
Below view, it is kicking.
To them I am nothing but shadow,
shape without substance.

With jealousy so sharp and shame
so blinding, I must turn my head and
view myself in gray against the wall.

This Dream Never Ends

Then tonight I drive your Laramie blue sedan
through the desert
You rock and hum,
holding tight our third passenger

Emerging from the station
you hand me the keys
and the lit image of the disappearing station
rolls forward into the windshield

The snake night swallows us like whole eggs

First Day in San Francisco

Who said anything about love?
We are living by the heart,
we are outlaws now.
We are by choice and by chance on
the same bench on
the same street in
the same San Francisco,
and I am crying into my hands
and you don't know me at all
so you don't ask me why.

I am crying because I'm finally
seeing the Golden Gate Bridge, and I'm not
soaring above it; I'm
sitting on a bench and
so helpless to move
and I'm waiting for my laundry to
spin-dry across the street,
seemed as good a day as any to
wash, this afternoon.
We came into this city stinking,
reeking of weeks
of highway and what was I thinking?

I was thinking you might have been
the one who would ask me,
if I ever stooped to tears in your presence,
Why are you crying?
let alone,
What can I do to make you stop?

Thank You, Diane di Prima, For Writing in Questions

Who knew? You use the same words,
the same
formations of questions I have
made my signature
(or, it decided to stay)
Better yet—
let me see
I have no answers

Setting fact aside, letting
wonder round it out,
the vacancy of a womb filled with
loss, breathing into that
embarrassed, hung
space, like a missed period,
just before it drops
viscous, suspended, unfinished—
I thought.

When you leave it open,
it feels like birth
though I have but abused myself
to barrenness

We test hard each part of us
to be sure
what finally springs forth,
what may or may not be answered,
is at least truly ready to be born.

Reckoning

She has reality
backed up like a tiger
against a steel fence.

Who is stronger?

Waking up in Samuel Taylor State Park, Surrounded by Redwoods

Reflections on the Hepcats Ball, 10/29/03
Great American Music Hall, San Francisco

In the morning as you sleep
I eat a sour apple we picked yesterday
off a tree on one of the trails.
Last night we slept in her womb,
woke in the vibratory hum of
Her Majesty,
echo of the Big Bang.

The tears of Allen Cohen,
as he read "The Last Days of Peace"

Phil Lesh, smiling,
almost fucking up the words to
yet another "Tom Thumb's Blues"—

Merl Saunders, post-stroke,
leaning heavily on his companion,
leaning heavily into his cane

Ram Dass, already "stroked,"
white-haired Aloha flower-bearer
silently mouthing new gems
(old reminders)
that want desperately to get to us,
poised to hear their wisdom:
"The Soul is carried by Love."

"Speak louder,"
someone shouted.
"Listen harder,"
someone replied.

The love we are conscious of receiving,
a slice of sunlight through a
redwood canopy.
Only a speck in what is actual,
what is tidal, oceanic.

Stray Cat on Speedball Alley

She hovers in the doorway,
waiting to pounce.
Her howls bounce off the walls and
closed windows of the
buildings above.
Once upon a time
those guys would all fuck her;
now, no one even lets her come up.
People eat at cafés
next to the dumpster,
stuffing their faces
full of the Hedra.
Watching, like it was another
Hollywood scene, and thinking,
She shouldn't get so upset;
it's bad for the baby.

Venice Is a Vampire

Men try to talk to me when I go outside.
Each one wants
whatever I will give.
The beach prowls with wolves,
swirls like a giardia-infested cesspool.

They ask me how I like the weather,
tell me how pretty I would look
if I weren't so angry.
Their eyes on my coconuts,
hanging ripe from my palms.

I keep my eyes on the ocean
until they leave.

I am just a hole
they are trying to squirm into.
Their tongues drip,
like they have found their way in,
are licking their fingers already.

    —laughing mad shadows grasp at my back as I
        walk away—

Venice is a vampire
hanging out at the end of the street,
naked under a trench coat in the rain.

On a good day here,
my heart wants to burst.
When it's gray,
I make myself appear empty,
hollow as the sewage pipe
with nothing inside
to be able
to suck out.

The Trees at the End of Westminster

The trees at the end of
Westminster
are good for leaning

leaning against and
watching

those who don't know they're
being watched

and those who do

Sestina

So, your ex called about the albums
said she saw them in a dream
and me, above them, posing
as the destructrix of the last memories,
the last tangible reminders of you two together.
She wants them out of our house.

Deep, hidden in the back room of our house
sit, gagged and silent, the rows of albums
that document your time together.
And so, as in her telltale dream,
I crack open the book of memories
and find her, half-naked and posing.

I think, how careless of her to be posing
for me in a new, unknown house
and I wonder if we will create new memories
that will one day fill scores of albums.
I always held fast to my dream
that I would be half of one, us together.

Years of your life, stacked neatly together,
people who didn't know they were posing,
only knew they were living a dream
grabbing from each room of the house
snapshots of laughter to the backdrop of albums—
the stuff that, in moments, creates memories.

Without evidence, I hold fast to my memories
and your body when we are together
I amass, haplessly, my past into mental albums
where I am the one who is posing
without a care in whose house
will exist the reminder of a night's sullen dream.

Was I burning them, in her dream?
Hacking apart the flimsy, half-forgotten memories
that suggest themselves worthy of moving to a house
where she and they could reunite together—
a vision fulfilled: Me, alone, posing
as the force that would hinder the use of those albums?

Let her dream about the albums.
We supersede your memories of her posing
in this house where we are now together.

Notes on a Sharon Olds Reading

What you said hangs from
four corners of a room,
like milk—
viscous,
ready to drop.

It does not belong
in a squared-off room,
nor a concrete one,
but one with flesh for walls,
rounded as a mother's hip,
or your own, deliberate curved lip
placed upon her pale cheek.

You take us, hushed and waiting
into the dry corners of her
parched mouth—
usher us in, whispering
spectators to the curious.

How the dead refuse to be discarded!
Even after ashes, the knell
echoes into the hollow
of months that follow—
and later, when we are home,
we touch our own skins,
figure out how to love despite
the inevitability of ashes.

This is the only way to love:
with skin
(knowing life goes on in its absence)
and
amidst a room full of strangers—
(knowing it continues in full
because of both).

New New Jersey Blues

From high above even California,
I see through the window of a New Jersey Transit car,
look down onto intersections in
Newark and Linden,
hear the orchestra of
5 a.m. garbage pick-up and
bakery deliveries
from Hoboken, Orange, Passaic Park

I see behind the storefronts of
Liquor Deli and Watch Repair,
Edison windows smeared with
lottery promises and pork roll grease
Metuchen diner parking lots open into
Rahway houses-become-bars,
Woodbridge Cadillacs, yawning at daybreak,
Elizabeth bungalows built up around the platform
and Amboy hospitals named for
Catholic saints
my grandmother hung above us
as we slept

Polish immigrants and their Hungarian children
Crocheted sofa covers, tattered awnings
God Bless America signs in Middlesex windows
Yellow ribbons tied around thin poplars
so no one forgets
   World War II and
   Desert Storm
      —still no one mentions Vietnam—

Routine of families like
meat, hanging off the bone,
edges brittle but hard,
like rusting iron
Hear they put up some more

Big Buildings on Route 18
Hear they put up another
Pharmaceuticals Mansion
in New Brunswick

Hope they keep Cook College
where you can still learn how to farm,
how to feed
all the mouths left hungry by the bridging of cities
lining the mouth of the Raritan
Hope they keep Waterloo Village
and its poetry festival for high schoolers,
keep the roads open to the Water Gap
where you can see the sunrise over the
New York City skyline, still visible from the
Appalachian Trail

When I close my eyes I can still take 287
out where there are horses
When I close my eyes I take the back roads through
Piscataway, where there are still
arrowheads in the dirt
Where what our parents and grandparents came to
and started as
still exists in the eyes of animals
and the sharpness of flint

November 2003 Harmonic Concordance

back door woman

feel like
running away
feel like
running to a foreign country
feel like
setting up a typewriter
at a window in
medjugorje
and pecking away at the
madonna
until i see her
face in my
words

feel like
smoking rolled
cigarettes
drinking stale
wine
alone
on a back porch in summer
after breathless
sex in a bedroom of
candles on the sill
mattress on the floor

feel like
going back
to the woman who would
do anything

wonder where
she went
wonder where
i put her

Yerma

after Lorca

Though she is young and
drops of water dart like
moonbeams on her arms,
she kneels with the washerwomen,
to wash what has not been used,
to wash what needs no washing at all.

The mouth of the river is the
solar plexus,
the inner sun where birds
sing at night,
not fearful of predators or
darkness.
Its mouth is full of honey,
its arms, stalks of wheat
its thighs, mountains whose sides
are cooled by a stream
whose source hides in clouds.

For Yerma, it is a sad day.
She speaks with a mouthful of
Jasmine, her womb is heavy and rich
and bitter as silt in the riverbed.
Dormant, waiting for the day that doesn't come,
her hopes pass over pebbles,
constant rivulets surrounding,
stripping slowly the faces of the stones
without ever knowing what we call years,
lifetimes.

Journeywoman

after Joy Harjo

I follow the path of instinct.
I have not been here
in this capacity.

Nights are still dark and
I'm scared to be alone.

The sky is always the
color of screams and silence.

The roof of my mouth
tastes metal,
the size of the light off
a cat's eye.

The new grass has been lightly trodden
by those who dare to tread by daylight.

I am of the first
to put my steps to rhythm,
governed by the distant sound of water,
the promise of fire.

A woman stops at the side of the road.

She places her baby on the ground.

The wolf waits at the edge of the forest.

The woman, the wolf, the baby.

All instincts are one:
long as dreams,
sharp as night vision.
I gather strength from the four corners.

I exhale fire and make the sky.

I build a crude wagon and join you on the
waterless river
to return to the place
that loved us,
that we destroyed
with our forgetting.

An Exceptional Poem

This happens every time
we read a poet we like.
We remember we have something
to remember,
to give, to expand.

We wish we would not censor.
We know nothing of the
bleeding that has occurred.

There burns the shining
gem of jealousy.

How it pulses on its throne—
anger's clitoris!

(acknowledgement to Robert Hayden)

I didn't want to be an English teacher,
I cried to Milton, again tonight.
He, sighing, asks,
Well, what did you want to be?

This night I read Gary Snyder,
"The Bath," from Turtle Island
and write back, to thank him
for prying open
the ancient, murmuring river of self,
revealing the Divine in
daily deeds,
reverberations from the past,
that root us, with words,
deep into the land we tread,
discard, ignore.

She has so much to tell us.
Holding my father and myself up on a ridge
at the lip of a rainforest of redwoods,
Sequoia sempervirens, ever-living big trees,
ever-silent, observing our silliness—
hurrying to catch the bus,
running all over in our desire to
be still with each other.

San Francisco, Muir Woods,
Napa Valley, Carmel, Santa Cruz,
San Luis Obispo (sleeping
giants on 101 blocked the ocean—
it roared and was angry and
we were no match for it)
and, suspended in the pelvic sling—
--LOS ANGELES—

I told Milton,
*I'm going to spend the night at
my parents' hotel.*
And finally, after she explained
to me how to sew an apron using
a sample pattern made from a napkin,
I crawled into her bed
and held her small, cotton
night-shirted body,
laid on her chest,
(flat now over ten years)
and wept into her collarbone
and felt sorry we had ever argued
It would be the last I would
hold her for some unknown time.

When I came here,
I wasn't conscious of time
and now I miss my mother and father.

I ripped myself from them so hard,
the waves are just beginning to settle.

So this is life, this is
living with someone,
this is opening, this is
having him inside me,
this is moving together,
preparing a space for a
new life—
somehow,
I had a different vision.

I was going to transform
the world, not
    be an English teacher.

My mother used to open the blinds
for me in the morning,

even then so reticent to rise
(I ask Milton to do it but he almost always
forgets and he most certainly does not sing,
Rise and shine and give God your glory, glory)

And what lesson did I think I didn't learn—
what do I know about
   how to love and
   how to give?

Finding the answers in
every new morning,
ever-shortening days.
Seeing angels at Pico and La Brea,
on the beach in Venice—
Get God on the phone:

Okay,
   we're ready for a new one
   down here...

To fold into our tribe,
kiss her awake,
sing sleep from her eyes as I
let the sunshine in

Acknowledgements

"New New Jersey Blues" first appeared
at Spiral Bridge Writers Guild.

"Stray Cat on Speedball Alley" first appeared
in *The Free Venice Beachhead.*

About the Author

Joy Rosenberg moved to California in 2000 after a young life on the east coast. Her poems and short stories have appeared in *The Free Venice Beachhead*, in the literary magazine *You*, at the New Jersey-based Spiral Bridge Writers Guild, and at Los Angeles Poet Society, where she was the winner of the 2016 Women's Poetry Month contest. She holds a Bachelor of Arts in religion from Wellesley College and a Master of Professional Writing from the University of Southern California, teaches in Los Angeles public schools, and lives at the beach with her husband and daughter.

www.ingramcontent.com/pod-product-compliance
Lightning Source LLC
Chambersburg PA
CBHW032050290426
44110CB00012B/1027